Relics of W

C000214343

A Guide to the 20th Century Military in the Northumberland Landscape

Contents

If you have anything of interest relating to the contents of this book, including corrections, additional information and anecdotes, please get in touch at:

books@wildsofwanney.co.uk

Introduction

When I look back to my childhood, both world wars still seemed to be in the recent past and not really thought of as history. There were stories in the family of Zeppelins over Bedlington during the first war, with Home Guard roadblocks and beaches covered in barbed wire in the second.

I knew about the wartime relics dotted around the local countryside. There was the old pillbox on the side of a railway bridge, and another by the canal. And there were the old air raid shelters on the school playing field that we were forbidden to enter.

After moving to Morpeth in the 1980s I became aware of the occasional pillbox on the back road to Mitford but it was when I came across an isolated pillbox, miles from anywhere, near Eglingham that my curiosity was finally aroused sufficiently to start investigating the "what" and "why" of all these constructions. And the more I looked into what was done during the six years of the second war, the more astounding it all became.

Once I started looking at Second World War remains the threads tended to lead both backwards to the period of the First World War and forwards to the Cold War. It became very apparent that the countryside is full of the relics of the military in the twentieth century.

I soon found out that, while other parts of the country had quite a lot of published material on the subject of military remains, there was very little about Northumberland. So this is an attempt to partly fill that gap; to provide an overview of the twentieth century military remains that can still be found in the Northumberland countryside and to try to put them into some historical context.

So what military remains can still be found in Northumberland? Well, apart from the defended beaches and the pillboxes (more than 200), there are trench systems from the first war, numerous coastal and anti-aircraft gun sites, radar stations, airfields, live firing ranges, underground "resistance" bases and cold war bunkers. Not bad for a county miles from the so-called centre of the action!

Ian Hall

The First World War

The First World War (WW1) is remembered mostly for the horrors of the trenches. While the conflict was much wider than the Western Front, the images of the battles in France and Flanders continue to resonate within our collective memories. Every town and village has its memorial to those who went to fight and never returned. Today, it is hard to imagine what effect this must have had in communities up and down the country.

So, although all the battles were fought overseas, what was happening at home and is there anything remaining on the ground here in Northumberland? Compared to the Second World War (WW2) there are not a lot of remains. But there are three sites which give an insight into different aspects of WW1.

Ashington Landing Field

On the home front there was none of the mass bombardment of civilians that would be seen in WW2. There were regular raids by airships and aeroplanes along the east coast and London was quite heavily bombed. Compared to what would happen in the future these attacks caused relatively little loss of life, but they did create a lot of public unrest.

Northumberland didn't see any raids by bomber aircraft; their range was such that they could only effectively reach targets in the south. The region did, however, suffer attacks by airships. In 1915 a Zeppelin passed over Blyth, dropping bombs at West Sleekburn. The following year three separate raids saw Zeppelins near Cresswell, Holy Island and Alnmouth. In all these cases, although bombs were dropped, little damage occurred.

These air raids prompted the creation of home defence squadrons. There was no shortage of aeroplanes for this purpose. The rapid development of the front line aeroplanes ensured that there was a steady supply of older machines for home defence. While no longer effective against the most modern German fighters these aircraft, such as the BE2 and FE2b, were still capable of combating the slow flying airships and bombers.

The home defence squadrons operated from simple grass landing fields. There would have been temporary buildings and tents for workshops but few, if any, permanent buildings. Within Northumberland airfields were established at a number of places, including Cramlington, Ashington [1], Alnwick and Haggerston. In addition seaplanes operated from Lindisfarne and Seahouses.

The only remaining evidence of these sites is at Ashington, where the remains of buildings that were built can be found beside the adjacent road [NZ246882].

1: An aerial view of the Ashington landing field showing the cross-shaped wood that was planted to help returning pilots find their way back [NZ240880].

Fort Coulson Coastal Guns

During this period the Royal Navy was the largest and best equipped in the world. It was therefore with some surprise that the German Navy was able to bombard the east coast towns of Hartlepool, Whitby and Scarborough in December 1914. Britain depended on its coastal shipping and these attacks prompted plans for defending the main ports and the important shipping lanes.

At this time, Blyth was a major port, shipping coal from the mines of South East Northumberland to London. In order to provide a defence against attacks a coastal gun installation, Fort Coulson [2], was built to the south of the town. It wasn't completed until 1918, however, too late to have any active role in the war.

2: Fort Coulson with one of the main gun batteries in the foreground and the WW2 Battery Observation Post behind [NZ320793].

The site had two emplacements, each with a six inch gun. There were also a number of supporting buildings including a Battery Observation Post for directing the fire of the guns, a magazine and two searchlights.

The site was decommissioned in 1924. It was then refurbished during WW2 and remains as an intact relic of both wars.

Further to the south a pair of coastal guns were built to protect the Tyne, at Marsden near South Shields and at Hartley near Seaton Sluice. These used the complete twelve inch turret assemblies from the decommissioned battleship HMS Illustrious. These batteries were not completed until after the end of war and were decommissioned in 1920s.

The gun at Hartley was called Roberts Battery [NZ342759]. Nothing remains on the surface of the main gun batteries. The gun control facility still exists as a house, Fort House, and two blockhouses and a water tower can be found in the immediate area.

Also, parts of the underground facilities can apparently be seen from the shore, where they have been exposed by the collapse of the cliff.

Rothbury Trenches

The battles fought on the western front were a new form of warfare, with trenches forming a continuous line from the Belgian coast to the Swiss border. Soldiers had to learn new skills in order to be able to live and fight in these new conditions. As regiments were prepared for battle, practice areas were created where the new recruits could see a little of what life would be like once they were at the front.

There is an area of moorland to the north of Rothbury where there are the remains of one of these practice areas [3]. On the ground the walls of trenches have slumped, but enough remains for the zig-zag layout to be clearly visible. There is also a similar trench area at Otterburn. Unfortunately this is within the current MoD range area and access would need to be arranged with the authorities [NT834026]. Otterburn was opened as an Army training area in 1911, and it has been operating continuously since then.

3: An aerial view of part of the practice trench system near Rothbury [NU049034].

When the war ended in November 1918, the losses had been so great that the whole nation wanted the Great War to be the "war that ended war". No-one wanted any repeat of what they had witnessed. Unfortunately within twenty years the peace in Europe was again to be shattered.

The Second World War

The Second World War (WW2) was the first truly global war, with most countries being affected in one way or another. It was a period of "total war" where every corner of Britain was involved in some way and it has left the biggest mark in the landscape. During the six years of the conflict there was a prodigious amount of construction work carried out, much of which still remains. Surprisingly, however, there are few official records which describe what was built during this period and why. It is only relatively recently that research has uncovered the complexity of the various plans that were being implemented.

The Gathering Clouds

During the 1930s the British armed forces were maintained at a minimal level. The general view was that the country wouldn't be fighting any more big wars with our European neighbours. Both the Army and RAF were kept small and poorly equipped; the RAF was still reliant on outdated biplanes for example. Only the Navy maintained its size in its role in policing the Empire, even if many of its ships had become outdated.

The militarisation of Germany during this period did finally awake the British government to the likelihood of another war. Belated attempts were made to update the armed forces, in particular the RAF. Luckily the outbreak of war was delayed sufficiently so that some measure of modernisation was achieved.

It had been recognised that air power would be a major factor in the future. The Spanish Civil War, where German and Italian aircraft were used against civilians, provided a foretaste of what we might expect here in Britain.

By 1937 Britain had a pair of modern fighter aircraft, the Hurricane and Spitfire. New air bases were built up and down the country, both as operational bases and for training. The first new airfield in Northumberland was RAF Acklington, which was built on the site of a WW1 landing field, Southfields [NU230000]. It was originally intended as an armament training camp, opening in 1937. On the outbreak of war, however, it was transferred to Fighter Command where it became the North East's main fighter base, initially flying Gloster Gladiator biplanes. These were soon replaced with Spitfires and Hurricanes.

As the war progressed, the Luftwaffe raids switched from day to night. Acklington then became home to various night-fighter squadrons, flying Defiants and Mosquitoes amongst other types.

This airfield has since disappeared due to open cast mining. A few of the original airfield buildings are still in use within the prison, HMP Northumberland, though these are clearly not accessible to the public!

Outside the perimeter of the prison there are a few remnants of the wartime airfield, including parts of the perimeter track and a number of airfield defence pillboxes [4].

At the same time as the RAF was being modernised, a team led by Robert Watson-Watt was developing a system for detecting approaching aircraft. In 1935 they made the first demonstration of a new technology that would become known as radar.

By the outbreak of war Britain had an operational radar system that covered the whole of the east coast, from the south of England to the north of Scotland. This was named Chain Home (CH). It was less advanced than the radar that had been developed by the Germans. The real achievement of the British system was, however, how information from the CH radar stations was integrated with visual reports from the Observer Corps and then coordinated by the RAF controllers who could talk directly with airfields and pilots.

There was one CH station built in Northumberland, at Ottercops Moss, near Elsdon. To the south the next CH station was at Danby Beacon, east of Guisborough, and to the north at Drone Hill near Coldingham in Scotland.

Incidentally, Ottercops Moss was the first radar station to track the flight of Rudolph Hess on 10th May 1941, when he flew to Britain in an unsuccessful attempt to broker a peace deal.

The CH sites all had a similar layout. The following plan [8] shows the main features of the Ottercops Moss site. There were three steel transmission masts, each 360 feet high, in a line parallel to the coast and four wooden receiving masts, each 240 feet high, arranged in a rhomboid shape to the side of the transmission masts. These masts no longer exist.

4: An airfield defence pillbox at RAF Acklington. There is a raised wall around the top, with a mounting for a light anti-aircraft gun on the roof.

5: Inside one of the type 22 pillboxes at the Ottercops Moss Chain Home radar site. These markings would have helped the occupants determine the range of any attackers.

6: One of the shell-proof pillboxes at the Ottercops Moss radar station. These are all in a poor condition, with much of the steel reinforcement exposed.

7: The sliding concrete roof of the reserve receiving station at Ottercops Moss [NY951895]. The transmission station is nearby [NY944898].

There are a number of supporting buildings which remain, however, including the gatehouse and the officer's mess, which is now in use as a house.

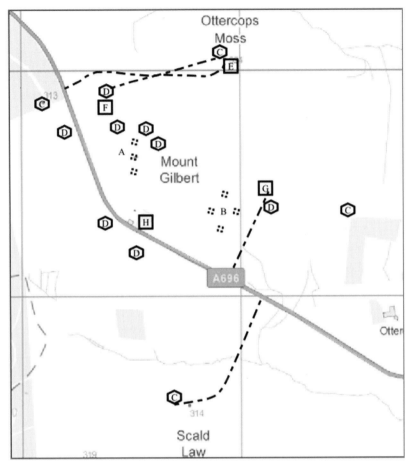

8: A plan of the Ottercops Moss radar station. This shows transmission masts [A], receiving masts [B], type 22 pillboxes [C], shell-proof pillboxes [D], anti-aircraft gun site [E], reserve transmission [F] and receiving [G] stations and gatehouse [H].

The site had four light anti-aircraft (LAA) positions, which would have probably used the 40mm Bofors gun. The foundations of one of these positions, together with the base of a hut, can be found [NY949900]. Each LAA position was protected by a type 22 pillbox which were manned by the regular Army. Their graffiti, including names and regiments, can be seen on the inside. There are also some markings which give the distance to landmarks which would have helped the occupants determine the range of any attacking force [5].

There are eight shellproof pillboxes which provided perimeter protection for the site, though these are all in a poor condition [6].

Surprisingly the Luftwaffe initially neither recognised CH sites as radar nor understood the British system of fighter control and so made few efforts to destroy any of the country's radar masts. The few attacks that did take place in the south of England were in the mistaken belief that these were radio broadcast masts. These attacks did, however, prompt the construction of underground reserve transmitting and receiving stations at many radar sites. These would have provided a back-up to the main over-ground facilities in case they were put out of action. They were fitted with concrete sliding roofs, the larger being for equipment installation and the smaller for personnel access [7].

So by the outbreak of WW2 Northumberland had one active fighter airfield and a radar station. How much more would be built in the following six years?

The Battle for Britain

Britain and France declared war on Germany on 3rd September 1939. The Army and RAF moved into France. Although there was fighting in other theatres, such as Norway, in France nothing happened until May 1940 when the German forces advanced rapidly through Western Europe. The British and French forces could do little to slow them and in less than a month the remnants of the Army had been evacuated from Dunkirk. The effectiveness of the Blitzkrieg tactics took the Allies totally by surprise and, with France fallen, Britain was faced with the unthinkable scenario of invasion.

Up until the Dunkirk evacuation there had been very little anti-invasion planning carried out. The immediate response therefore drew on the traditional strategy of that time which involved static defence lines. These were intended to slow down or halt the advancing enemy, while allowing reinforcements to be brought to bear at the required locations. It was this thinking that had led, for example, to the construction of the Maginot line in France. And so began a massive construction programme which would affect the whole of Britain.

On the coast, this defence line strategy was known as Coastal Crust. The "crust" was a continuous, but thin, line of defences along all vulnerable coastlines. Public access to beaches was prohibited, with the shoreline being strewn with barbed wire and mines. Scaffolding was erected below the high tide line to deter landing craft.

The concrete anti-tank cubes which formed part of the crust are, perhaps, the most visible and well known part of the Northumberland anti-invasion defences. These blocks were normally laid out in double rows with barbed wire strung between them. While the blocks can still be seen on many of the beaches in the county, over time many have been buried by the shifting sands, moved by tides and storms and relocated to create new defences against coastal erosion.

In addition to the blocks small machine gun posts were built on the beaches, normally using concrete filled sandbags. Time has not been kind to these and most can now only be seen as piles of rounded concrete blocks.

There are a couple of great examples of how all of this would have looked in 1940, at the Lindisfarne causeway [front cover] and at Cheswick [11]. At these locations everything has been protected from the worst effects of nature and you can see the concrete blocks in rows, remnants of the barbed wire fastenings on the blocks and well preserved machine gun posts.

The risk of invasion by glider-borne troops was understood and a series of anti-glider defences were constructed. On some of the larger beaches old cars were filled with stones and staked to the sand below the high water line. Though most of these have been removed or have corroded away, remnants can sometimes be found at Bamburgh and Beadnell, particularly after heavy storms.

In other areas, such as the mud flats to the north of the Lindisfarne causeway, anti-glider poles were erected [NU090440]. Remarkably, some of these have remained in position.

Also anti-glider and anti-tank ditches were dug near the coast, though these have in the main been filled in.

The coastal defences were completed with a series of pillboxes and gun emplacements built close to the shore. Gun emplacements housed larger guns and were usually built at the ends of beaches where they could provide enfilading fire along the shoreline.

Good examples of such emplacements survive at Scremerston [9] and Budle Bay [NU161357]. Some are quite dilapidated like the collapsed emplacement found at the base of the cliff near Longhoughton [NU261158]. Others are almost completely buried in sand, as at Warkworth [NU254079].

9: Gun emplacement at Scremerston [NU031480].

There are also the remains of a number of gun emplacements along the coast to the north of Newbiggin-by-the-Sea, with a particularly impressive set of defences near Lynemouth power station [12].

Many of these emplacements housed old naval guns as more modern weapons were still in short supply. There are also stories of telegraph poles being used as imitation gun barrels in order to deceive enemy reconnaissance flights.

At the same time that the coastal defences were being built a series of inland stop lines was being constructed. These would be brought into play should the coastal defences be breached. These lines made use of existing landscape features wherever possible, such as hills, rivers and canals. They were made up of pillboxes to provide strong points with newly constructed barriers such as anti-tank ditches. All of this was intended to slow, and hopefully halt, the advance of an invading force.

The main spine of this inland system was planned at a national level and was called the GHQ line. Local area commanders were given the task of augmenting this backbone, using their specific local knowledge. It was partly by such delegation that so much was built in such a short time. It was recognised that all of these inland lines could not be fully manned, the plan being instead to occupy positions as necessary to counter the specific invasion threat that might emerge.

Northumberland's main defence lines made use of the Coquet and Wansbeck rivers. The pillboxes in both lines were constructed to the south of the rivers and are well preserved. They were intended to eventually provide a defence line from the Cheviot Hills to the coast, where they would have linked to the "coastal crust". The Coquet Stop Line starts at the edge of the hills, near Hepple, with a pillbox every mile or so, though it does peter out near Felton. The Wansbeck Stop Line seems never to have extended further west than Meldon and there is little to be seen east of Morpeth.

Supporting these main stop lines, two subsidiary lines were built to the north of the Coquet, between Wooler and Belford, and Wooler and Alnwick. These two lines have survived almost complete.

The stop-line strategy was, however, starting to raise some concerns at a national level due to its essentially static nature. One of the major failings was that once breached in a single place, the whole line became vulnerable. Following a single break through the enemy could either bypass or encircle the remaining defences.

Also, some of the stop lines seem to be ill-conceived. As an example, although the Wooler/Alnwick line crosses the Great North Road, none of the pillboxes provided any defence to this principal route.

You could believe that the lines had been designed miles away by someone drawing a line on a map, taking no account of local conditions. We shouldn't be too critical of this, however, as the whole strategy was developed and implemented within a few weeks of the Dunkirk evacuation.

In July 1940 General Brooke, newly returned from France, was given the task of reorganising the nation's defences. He was able to bring in his first hand experiences from the Battle of France where he had seen how the Blitzkrieg tactics relied on the rapid movement of troops, mainly along existing roads rather than across open land.

The defence plan was rapidly amended and the focus of inland defence lines was switched to one of defending key towns, road junctions and bridges [13]. This would still fulfil the aim of slowing down the advance of any invading force, but the defences would be more robust; the loss of one part of a defensive ring would not inevitably lead to the collapse of the whole. The experience of France had shown that defending a town was easier than defending open countryside.

This new strategy took the name of "nodal point" defence and, where possible, the defence lines were adapted to meet this new plan. At the same time, much of the actual manning of these defences was put over to the newly established Home Guard battalions, who could now operate within their own town or village. The Regular Army would then be released to reinforce the area where an invasion had actually occurred. This change in strategy presumably explains why the river stop lines was never fully completed.

This new approach led to the construction of defences around key towns. Locally, these defended locations included the towns of Wooler, Alnwick, Belford and Morpeth. The defences included pillboxes, many of which still survive [14]. There would also have been roadblocks at each road entrance into these towns, though no evidence of these remains.

Buildings and walls were modified to provide loopholes for specific defensive roles, such as protecting roadblocks.

In Alnwick, the cemetery wall has a series of loopholes which would have protected the south entrance into the town [NU195121]. Loopholes can also be seen in a wall on the Canongate [NU181139], as well as in the wall of a building overlooking the Lion Bridge [NU185137].

In other areas, loopholes can be clearly seen on the south side of the Telford Bridge in Morpeth[NZ201858], at Bothal [NZ239866] and Ulgham [NZ232923].

That the vast majority of these defences were constructed in a period of less than four months is a staggering feat that must have involved a large part of the population and probably the majority of building contractors up and down the country. The amount of construction was so great that national shortages of concrete were being reported at times during 1940.

Nationally, a standard set of pillbox designs was developed by the War Office Fortifications and Works Department 3. These were all given the designation FW3, but were not widely used in Northumberland, where the majority of the defences were constructed by local commanders using their own designs. Where these national designs were used, it was mainly at sites outside the remit of local commanders, such as airfields and radar stations.

A common FW3 design is the type 22 which can be recognised by being a regular hexagon in plan, with sides of about two metres long. Inside there was an anti-blast wall which would provide protection to occupants from ricochets and concrete fragments.

10: These shaped concrete blocks can often be found around lozenge pillboxes. They would have been used to reduce the size of larger embrasures.

Of the local designs, the most common is the "lozenge" [15]. In plan, this is an elongated hexagon construction with an entrance porch to the rear, embrasures on all sides and with an internal anti-blast wall. Shaped concrete blocks can often be found near these pillboxes which would be used to reduce the size of the larger embrasures; the larger openings were used for automatic weapons, such as the Bren, and the smaller for rifles [10]. The stepped form of the gun embrasures reduced the chances of any attacker's bullets being deflected into the pillbox.

Another common local design also has six sides but with a flat rear face, creating a "D" shaped plan form. Examples of these can be found in a number of locations including parts of the Wooler to Belford line and at Eglingham village, which is defended by three such pillboxes.

A few other more unusual designs exist, including simple concrete filled sand-bags pillboxes [14], pre-fabricated pillboxes [16] and camouflaged pillboxes, disguised as cottages for example [17].

While all the anti-invasion work was being undertaken, work was also being done to bring Fort Coulson back into operation. Blyth was still an important coal port, so in 1940 the facility was refurbished and two new six inch guns were installed. A new Battery Observation Post (BOP) was also built, housing modern ranging equipment. This can still be seen alongside the earlier BOP from WW1 [2].

The final, and most secret, element of the country's defence strategy were the Auxiliary Units. There were two discrete branches of this organisation and they were to be brought into action if the enemy managed to establish a strong foothold within Britain.

The first branch of the Auxiliary Units was established to carry out sabotage behind the advancing enemy lines. Each Unit was made up of about four to six local men. People who had a good knowledge of the land were preferred, such as farmers, fishermen, game keepers and poachers. They were given intensive training and provided with the most up-to-date weaponry and explosives. Sworn to secrecy, and wearing Home Guard uniforms as part of their cover, it is only relatively recently that families of those involved have discovered what their relatives had been committed to do.

Each unit was provided with an underground Operational Base. These were constructed in secrecy, normally in areas of woodland. The hides were to a standard design, looking a little like an underground air raid shelter, with a single room about six metres by two metres in size. They had a concealed entrance and an emergency escape tunnel exiting some distance away.

There were about eighteen Auxiliary Units in Northumberland, each with their own hide. Unfortunately most of the sites are in a very poor condition, either completely or partially collapsed. By their very nature they are difficult to find and all known examples are on private land [19].

The second branch of the Auxiliary Units was the Special Duties section. This was

11: Coastal crust anti-tank blocks at Cheswick, with a foundation for a gun position. The mounting bolts are still in place [NU050462].

12: A gun emplacement, together with defending pillboxes near Lynemouth [NZ311896].

13: Sandbag type pillbox at the south end of Bothal bridge [NZ236862].

14: Sandbag type pillbox to the south of the river Aln near Alnwick [NU200136].

15: Lozenge type pillbox on the Alnwick/Wooler stop line, built into the ramparts of Old Bewick hillfort [NU076216].

16: Pre-fabricated type pillbox near Dunstanburgh castle [NU257215].

17: Camouflaged pillbox at Druridge Bay [NZ283946].

18: Gloucester Lodge Heavy Anti-aircraft Battery. The four gun positions are in a semi-circle to the front of the site [NZ321785].

set up later than the sabotage units and was to be responsible for collecting and communicating intelligence about the deployment of the invading enemy.

Both men and women were involved in the Special Duties Auxiliary Units. In the main, they were recruited from people whose work would have allowed them relatively free movement, such as doctors, district nurses and vicars. They would prepare simple intelligence reports, based on what they had seen.

19: An interior view of one of the Auxiliary Unit Operational Bases in Northumberland. The entrance has collapsed and soil can be seen spilling into the main chamber.

These would be left in concealed "letter boxes"; under rocks, in holes in trees etc. The reports were then collected by the next level of operatives who would have access to a secret radio transmitter known as an out-station. These transmissions would be received by a local control station who would then relay them to the main military headquarters. Messages could also be dropped directly into these control stations [20]. This control station or "zero station" would be constructed in an underground hide, similar to, but larger than that used by the sabotage Auxiliary Units.

There is one example of a Special Duties "zero station" in the county, at Heiferlaw, north of Alnwick. This is in good condition, but it is on private land and not accessible to the public.

In the event of an invasion all the different bases would have been occupied. The Auxiliary Units would wait for the front line to pass over them and would then operate behind enemy lines, carrying out sabotage and intelligence gathering.

20: An inside view of part of the Heiferlaw Special Duties Zero Station. These two tubes would be connected to hidden locations on the surface. Agents would be able to drop messages into the underground base via these tubes.

In this way the aim was to make life very difficult for any invading force, and ultimately to be able to retake the initiative and so repel the enemy. Whether this would have been successful is now an academic question, but the very existence of the two parts of the Auxiliary Units demonstrated the lengths to which the anti-invasion preparations would go.

During all of this construction work the Battle of Britain was being fought in the skies of southern England. We now know that the failure of the Luftwaffe to achieve air superiority over the intended invasion beaches led to the postponement and then cancellation of Operation Sea Lion, the planned invasion of Britain. In 1941, the threat of invasion was further reduced when Germany invaded Russia.

The anti-invasion defences were kept active, however, as it was felt that there was a strong possibility that Russia could have been defeated. This would have probably resulted in Britain again coming under invasion threat. It is also possible that the government saw these anti-invasion activities as helping to keep the nation focused on the war, at a time when the Allies were not able to strongly engage with the enemy elsewhere.

But the immediate reduction in invasion risk allowed Britain to take stock and start to prepare to stabilise the position of the country.

Blood, Sweat and Tears

With the immediate threat of invasion reduced the country could start to dig in for the longer term. The main threat was now from air raids by Luftwaffe bombers. With most of the European coast line under German control, bombers could be sent to pretty much anywhere in the country. As a result, more aircraft were required and so more airfields needed to be built.

In 1941, a second Northumberland operational fighter airbase was opened; RAF Ouston [NZ080700] near Harlow Hill. A number of aircraft types were based there, including Spitfires and Hurricanes.

Airfields naturally became one of the main targets of bombing raids. In an attempt to protect against such attacks, decoy sites were built to try to divert bombers from attacking the real airfield. During the early stages, when attacks were mainly in the daylight, the decoys were dummy airfields. These had runways painted on the grass, together with plywood aeroplanes and buildings. These were known as K-sites. One was established at Boulmer as a decoy site for Acklington.

The RAF fighter aircraft considerably reduced the effectiveness of daylight bombing raids and as the Luftwaffe losses mounted so the bombing raids were switched to the night. The K-sites fell into disuse and new decoys, known as Q-sites, were developed. These used lighting effects to try to imitate the flare path of an active airfield. This approach was also used to protect major industrial targets, with sites known as QL or Starfish. Little remains of any of these sites other than the buildings which were used to control the lighting effects. The remains of the control buildings for the decoy sites for RAF Acklington and RAF Ouston can be seen, respectively near Widdrington [NZ262943] and Berwick Hill [NZ176757].

The other main defence against night raids was anti-aircraft guns, coupled with searchlights and barrage balloons.

The port of Blyth was protected by a number of heavy anti-aircraft gun positions. Of these only one remains, though it is remarkably complete. This battery is at Gloucester Lodge to the south of the town, where the four 3.7 inch gun emplacements are still visible together with the remains of the supporting buildings and the foundations of the barracks for the gun crew [18].

Searchlight and barrage balloon positions are harder to find as they leave little trace.

21: Craster Chain Home Low radar building with two of the four columns that supported the rotating dish clearly visible in the centre and right of the wall [NU255203].

By this time, the limitations of Chain Home radar were becoming very apparent and raiders were avoiding detection by flying low over the sea and "under the radar". A new system of radar was therefore developed, known as Chain Home Low (CHL). These stations were constructed nearer the coast and used the rotating aerials that we now associate with radar.

A number of CHL sites were built along the Northumberland coast and the remains of two of these, at Craster [21] and Scremerston [NU008501] can be seen. At both of these sites the two principal buildings remain. One housed the radar transmitting and receiving equipment, where the mountings for the rotating radar dish can be seen on the roof. The other building housed an electrical generator. Accommodation buildings were built close by.

The whole of the area around the Craster radar station has been investigated by archaeologists and a large number of wartime remains have been discovered, including gun pits, mine fields, and even gardens created by Italian PoWs who were held there later in the war.

The CHL sites were continually updated throughout the war as technology advanced, becoming CHEL (Chain Home Extra Low).

The Beginning of the End

By 1942 plans were being developed for the liberation of Europe. The USA had joined Britain, and American troops and airmen were gathering all across the country. The tide of the war was beginning to turn in favour of the Allies.

Northumberland's open skies, away from the more congested areas further south, made it an ideal area for the training of new RAF pilots. In 1942 four new airfields were opened in the county.

RAF Eshott [NZ180980], near Felton, housed an Operational Training Unit, training pilots to fly Spitfires. This was a single seat aircraft; only a very few two-seat versions were built. New pilots therefore had to take a leap into the unknown when they first took to the air in these high-performance machines, after very little flying training on more simple aircraft types.

At the airfield itself the runways are visible and many of the wartime accommodation buildings can be seen, particularly along the road down to Eshott Heugh. Parts of the perimeter track are still in use as roadways and some of the dispersal pads, where aircraft would be parked, can be seen. This airfield remains in use for private aircraft and microlights, utilising part of the old wartime runway.

RAF Milfield [NT950330] was built on the site of the Woodbridge WW1 landing field. This airfield was used for training pilots in ground attack, mainly using Typhoon and Tempest aircraft. Training for these types of operations was very important as they would be used in supporting troops on the ground in the days following D-Day. It was very dangerous, involving low flying at very high speeds. Although this airfield is still in use, primarily for gliding, there are few wartime remains to be seen. There was a decoy site for Milfield at Lowick but its exact location is not currently known.

RAF Brunton [24] was opened as a satellite to Milfield in order to accommodate the large numbers of aircraft that were needed for the training there. Brunton has been largely untouched and now represents the most complete WW2 airfield in the county. Unfortunately access to it is currently limited to a public right of way which crosses the end of one runway. There was a decoy site for Brunton at Elford, but as with Lowick, its exact location is unknown.

RAF Morpeth [NZ170820] was opened as an Air Gunnery School, training bomber air gunners. The gunners would be trained using the gun turrets in Avro Anson aircraft, firing at targets towed by Lysanders and Martinets at the Druridge Bay ranges. There are substantial remains at this site.

In 1943, the final Northumberland airfield was opened at RAF Boulmer [NU250130]. This site, initially a K-type decoy site for Acklington, was developed into a full airfield as a satellite for RAF Eshott. The runway has since been dug up, but its location can be seen in the fields.

At this period, airfields pretty much followed a standard design, with only minor adjustments to deal with local circumstances. There were usually three runways in a triangle arrangement to give the pilots the best chance of being able to land and take off into the wind. A perimeter track encircled the runways and linked a large number of circular dispersal points which were used to keep parked aircraft well separated to prevent them being an easy target for attackers. There was a wide range of support buildings for the airfield, including accommodation, administration, medical, stores and maintenance etc.

There might also be pillboxes for airfield defence. These can be found at Acklington and Ouston which, being the earlier airfields, were seen as potential landing sites for invading airborne troops during 1940/41. These often had their main embrasures facing towards the airfield in order to counter this invasion threat. Many airfields also had a Battle HQ bunker which would be brought into action in the event of the airfield being occupied by enemy troops. At Acklington, the defence pillboxes have an unusual design in that they have built up walls on top to provide an enclosed light anti-aircraft gun position [4].

Supporting all these training airfields was a large number of practice ranges where live ammunition could be used.

22: One of the two range towers at Cheswick. This one has been built on top of an older coastal crust pillbox [NU051462].

Druridge Bay became, in effect, one large target range, with the danger area extending well out to sea. This must have caused some restrictions for the local fishermen. A number of range buildings can still be seen in the dunes.

Cheswick and Goswick were used as ranges for air to ground target practice. The beaches were littered with various targets such as old vehicles, tanks and even railway locomotives. The beaches here can still reveal live ammunition from this period and there are rumours that one of the dunes on the beach is formed from the remains of the targets. Until recently a team of RAF bomb disposal experts was based here, carrying out regular clearances and controlled explosions. This work has now been taken over by civilians. Two range towers survive on the beach area, with one being built on top of an anti-invasion pillbox [22].

The coast near Ross was used as an artillery range. The site included a narrow gauge railway system that provided a moving target for anti-tank gunnery practice [23]. The marks made by the looping tracks of this system are visible on the ground.

There are also four structures associated with this system which would have housed range staff who would repair holes in the canvas targets as the train passed by [25]. The whole system was subsequently relocated to the Otterburn ranges [NT825017]. It is not possible to access most of the Ross area but a public footpath runs through the middle of the site to the beach, which allows a good overall view. The ground still bears the scars of the artillery explosions that occurred.

23: An aerial view of the remains of one of the looped tracks at Ross [NU141376].

Doddington Moor and Horton Moor, near Wooler, were used as ground attack ranges. Signs of the impact of bombs can be seen in places on the moorland. These ranges were only a few minutes flying time from the airfield at Milfield, which meant that the aircraft would be attacking their targets immediately after take-off. This turned out to be the situation that the pilots would often encounter in action, where they were operating from bases just behind the front line.

Also some of the old defence line pillboxes seem to have been used for target practice. The effects of machine guns on concrete is evident on pillboxes at Eglingham Moor [NU106204] and Bowden Doors [NU062331], where the walls have been badly damaged and remnants of bullets remain embedded in the concrete.

The flying training carried out in Northumberland was very dangerous and many pilots were killed, even before they went into action. There were also a lot of aircraft crashes during operational flights , both Allied and Luftwaffe. Many of the air crew who were killed were buried locally, where their graves continue to be

24: An aerial view of RAF Brunton showing the "A" arrangement of the runways which was typical of airfields of this time [NU210260].

25: Bunker at Ross which protected range staff who repaired the moving canvas targets that ran round the railway tracks [NU138375].

26: Some of the remains of the USAAF B-17 Flying Fortress that crashed on the slopes of The Cheviot. Two members of the crew were killed [NT894213].

27: The surface features at the Whittingham ROC base. To the right is the main access hatch, with the ventilation shaft to the left. Various detection instruments would have been attached to the tubes which emerge from the ground [NU074115].

maintained by the Commonwealth War Graves Commission.

The wreckage of crashed aircraft can still be found in the Cheviot Hills. One of these is that of a USAAF B-17 Flying Fortress which crashed on the slopes of The Cheviot after getting lost in bad weather when returning from a bombing raid [26]. Two of the nine air crew died in the crash, but the remaining crew were saved, mainly due to the efforts of two local shepherds and their dogs .

There is a memorial to all the wartime pilots who were lost in the Cheviots, in the College valley [rear cover].

VE Day and Beyond

When the war in Europe ended in May 1945 there was a rapid dismantling of most of the wartime military facilities.

RAF Acklington remained operational, eventually becoming the base for the air sea rescue helicopters of 202 squadron. It was finally closed in 1972, when the helicopters were transferred to RAF Boulmer.

RAF Ouston became a base for the Auxiliary Air Force, and in 1974 it was passed over to the Army to become Albemarle Barracks. As a result, it cannot be visited, though there are a number of pillboxes still in existence outside the secure boundary.

The radar stations were closed down, to be replaced by a new site at Boulmer.

Fort Coulson was closed, but has since been restored by a team of dedicated volunteers.

Most of the remaining facilities were simply abandoned.

The Cold War

The end of WW2 didn't bring the tranquillity that might have been hoped for. Very quickly the "iron curtain" descended across Europe. The lines were drawn for what became known as the Cold War. It was a period defined by international tensions and the prospect of nuclear Armageddon. Much of what happened during this period was done in total secrecy and it is only with the collapse of the Soviet Union that some of Britain's secrets have been allowed to emerge. Many of us lived through this period oblivious to much of what was happening.

The threat of attack was coming from the USSR. Initially this was from bomber aircraft and later from Intercontinental Ballistic Missiles (ICBM). The strategy at this time was given the very apt acronym MAD (Mutually Assured Destruction).

In order to be able to detect attacking aircraft the WW2 radar systems had to be improved and a new generation, called ROTOR, was developed. A number of sites were built along the east coast. It was at this time that the radar site at RAF Boulmer came into being as part of this network. This station remains in operation as part of Britain's air defence system.

As well as detecting a potential attack it was vital that any such threat could be rapidly and securely communicated through the NATO command structure. In a world before satellites such communication was not easy. Radio links relied on a clear line of sight between transmitting and receiving stations. Normal telephone lines were seen as being too vulnerable to disruption during a crisis.

In the late 1950s, a new system, known as Ace High, was developed which could transmit over very long distances by bouncing a signal off the troposphere layer of the atmosphere. The scattering of radio waves in this way was very inefficient and relied on both very powerful transmitters and very sensitive receivers to pick up the weak signals. The system was made to work, however, and it covered the entire NATO western boundary from Norway to Turkey. One of the 64 sites in this system was built at RAF Brizlee Wood near Alnwick [NY937644]. Ace High was eventually replaced by communication satellites. The Brizlee Wood site is still there, however, operating as part of the radar for RAF Boulmer. Its golf ball dome is clearly visible from many parts of the county.

Recognising the devastation that would be brought by a nuclear war, the British government sought ways to maintain some form of control of the surviving population. Reinforced bunkers were built where some form of government could be maintained after a nuclear attack. For the early period of the Cold War Northumberland was controlled from Catterick garrison but eventually in the 1970s a regional headquarters was established at Hexham. It was built in an old concrete WW2 cold store [NY937644]. This building has now been demolished.

Due to the perceived vulnerability of the telephone network, a robust microwave communication system was created across the UK. This was made up of a network of radio stations and it was built and operated by the General Post Office. Its primary use was for Civil Defence but it also carried normal civilian communications. The most iconic of these radio stations is the Post Office Tower in London.

One of these stations was built in Northumberland, at Corby's Crag near Alnwick [NU139100]. This site was part of the main backbone of the national system and it is still in operation, though no longer for Civil Defence.

In addition, a new role was established for the Royal Observer Corps, which had earned its Royal status in recognition of its role during WW2. Over 1500 underground posts were constructed throughout the country from where the spread of the effects of a nuclear strike could be monitored. The measurements that could be made included, for example, the direction and intensity of a nuclear blast and the residual radioactivity.

Teams of three or four members of the ROC would man these posts. In the event of an attack they would have had to remain underground for an extended period and so the posts had rudimentary accommodation, such as bunk beds and chemical toilets.

These ROC posts were built between 1957 and 1965 but were progressively decommissioned from 1968, with the final closures being in the early 1990s. The posts are all of a standard design and inside, many still have all their contents, as though they were just abandoned when shut down.

There were about 30 ROC posts in Northumberland, though only about half of these remain. Surviving examples are at Bamburgh [NU166350] and Whittingham [27].

Exploring Northumberland

Visiting Sites

This book does not aim to identify all the military remains within Northumberland. Indeed, sites are still being rediscovered. There should be enough references within the text and gazetteer, however, to allow anyone interested to explore this subject within the county. All the map references in this book, being "six-figure", define a location to within an area 100 metres square. In open land this is normally enough but in some cases a bit of exploring may be required before the remains can be found.

As a warning, be wary when visiting sites. Most of the structures have not been maintained since they were abandoned so care must be taken when approaching them. They can be dangerously unstable.

There are a number of places where a good selection of remains can be found in a relatively small area, and are therefore especially worthy of a visit.

Ottercops Moss. The site of a Chain Home radar station has a large number of different buildings. The ground is quite rough so good boots will be needed.

Dunstanburgh. In the area around the castle and Embleton Bay there are a number of coastal pillboxes as well as the Craster Chain Home Low radar station.

Blawearie. There are four pillboxes in hills in this area. There are also a number of archaeological remains, including hill forts and cup and ring marked stones, all of which make for an interesting walk.

Wooler. Two stop lines terminate here and there are the remains of the ring of pillboxes that once encircled the town.

Blyth. Fort Coulson has extensive remains from both World Wars and the Gloucester Lodge anti-aircraft site is just across the road.

Mapping websites, such as the Ordnance Survey, can be very useful as map references can be viewed directly on both maps and aerial photographs.

When out and about you may come across sites which aren't included in this book. The websites in the bibliography can help in determining what these remains might be.

Rights of Access

A right of access to any of the sites cannot be presumed. Visitors must make their own assessment prior to visiting each site, requesting permission from land owners as necessary.

Many of the sites are on public access land, as defined in the Countryside and Rights of Way Act. These areas are freely accessible though there may be local restrictions in force, for example relating to dogs.

Defence of Britain Project

Much of the information about WW2 remains was collected between 1995 and 2001 as part of the Defence of Britain Project. Members of the public were invited to submit information about any remains that they were aware of. The list that was created was not complete and it is still being added to. It did, however, provide the first real overview of the extent of the construction work carried out during WW2. The database can be accessed on the internet.

Acknowledgements and Thanks

I would like to thank the following for their help in getting this book published.

The Pillbox Study Group as a whole, and Colin Anderson and Stephen Lewins in particular, who have given freely of their vast knowledge.

Elaine, for her support, proof reading and general forbearance, when every walk for the past five years ended up at some pillbox or other.

The folks at Azure who helped me make the book a reality, and Purple Aviation, who flew me round to take the aerial photographs.

And last, but not least, thank you for buying this book. I hope that it has been of interest.

Gazetteer

Coastal Pillboxes

Beal Point	NU080433	Bamburgh	NU179354
Swinhoe	NU214285	Embleton Bay	NU246224
Boulmer	NU261144	Foxton	NU258120
Alnmouth	NU251110	Warkworth	NU251063

Coquet Stop Line Pillboxes –Hepple to Felton Section

Harehaugh	NT972999	Hepple	NT977000
Hepple	NY985998	Bickerton	NT993004
Bickerton	NU001007	Little Tosson	NU009014
Ryehill	NU022016	Newtown	NU036011
Carterside	NU046010	Rothbury	NU058015
Whitton	NU068004	West Raw	NZ087996
Pauperhaugh	NZ099993	Brinkburn	NZ114985
Brinkheugh	NZ126984	Weldon Bridge	NZ139983
Catheugh	NZ152993		

Wansbeck Stop Line Pillboxes – Mitford to Molesden Section

Mitford	NZ173858	Mitford Castle	NZ169854
Molesden	NZ144848	Molesden	NZ139842

Inland Pillboxes

Shilbottle	NU190067	Brainshaugh	NU202033
W Thirston	NZ190999	Earsdon	NZ203939

Belford-Wooler Stop Line Pillboxes

Weetwood Hill	NU011304	Broomy Knw	NU015309
Horton Moor	NU016315	Meakaill Knw	NU035318
Hetton Burn	NU046329	Raven's Crag	NU062331
Bowden Doors	NU073332	Blagdon Dean	NU088337

Alnwick-Wooler Stop Line Pillboxes

Loaning Head	NU191153	Heckley Hse	NU188164
Heiferlaw	NU179180	White House	NU162180
W Ditchburn	NU132202	Eg'ham Hill	NU119199
Eglingham	NU106204	Harehope	NU091208
Tick Law	NU084214	Old Bewick (2)	NU075215
Bewick Folly	NU062226	Bewick Bridge	NU052227
Ewe Hill	NU045244	Newtown	NU033258
Highcairn	NU019262	Tower Martin	NU010269

Nodal Point Defence Pillboxes

Wooler	NU004281	NT989276	NT984275
NT983278	NT984280	NT987284	NT993287
Alnwick	NU200136	NU206130	NU201134
Eglingham	NU109194	NU106196	NU104196
Morpeth	NZ192865	NZ198876	NZ189878
NZ216866	NZ213862	NZ175863	NZ176868

Airfield Defence Pillboxes

RAF Acklington	NU239003	NU224014	NU222007
RAF Ouston	NZ075695	NZ079705	NZ076687

Ottercops Moss Chain Home Radar Pillboxes

NY955894	NY947885	NY941899	NY949901
NY946897	NY944899	NY951894	NY944893
NY945892	NY942897		

Bibliography and Further Reading

Books

Defending Britain; Twentieth Century Military Structures in the Landscape; Osbourne M, Tempus 2004

The Military Airfields of Britain; Northern England; Delve K, Crowood 2006

Airfields of North-East England in the Second World War; Chorlton M, Countryside Books 2005

Cold War; Building for Nuclear Confrontation 1946 – 1989; Cockcroft W and Thomas J, English Heritage 2003

Air Crash Northumberland; Gray R, Corbett J, Shipley J, Anderson N, Countryside Books 2008

And finally, Volume 20 of Northumberland County Council's Archaeology in Northumberland has detailed articles on the Heiferlaw Zero Station and the Bamburgh ROC post.

Websites

Defence of Britain database: A searchable list of WW2 relics
http://ads.ahds.ac.Britain/catalogue/collections/blurbs/324.cfm

Pillbox Study Group: A volunteer group dedicated to researching WW2 relics
http://www.pillbox-study-group.org.Britain/

Subterranea Britannica: details of various underground buildings in the UK, together with details of the locations of all the ROC posts in Northumberland
http://www.subbrit.org.Britain/

British Resistance Archive: Details of the auxiliary units, including all the known AUOB sites in Northumberland
http://www.coleshillhouse.com/

Wilds of Wanney: home of Wanney Books and information about the history, heritage and countryside of Northumberland
http://www.wildsofwanney.co.uk/